IMAGES
of America

MEADVILLE'S ARCHITECTURAL HERITAGE

Nature's signature for the community, the rhododendrons signal the arrival of Memorial Day and the summer season. This view, looking south from Allegheny College's campus over the valley, conveys some sense of the display the shrubs provide. When Greendale Cemetery was designed in 1856, rhododendrons were an essential element of the plan, and today they are found at modest and elegant buildings throughout the community.

IMAGES
of America

MEADVILLE'S ARCHITECTURAL HERITAGE

Anne W. Stewart and Steven B. Utz

Published by Arcadia Publishing
Charleston SC, Chicago IL, Portsmouth NH, San Francisco CA

Printed in Great Britain

Library of Congress Catalog Card Number: 2005928680

For all general information contact Arcadia Publishing at:
Telephone 843-853-2070
Fax 843-853-0044
E-mail sales@arcadiapublishing.com
For customer service and orders:
Toll-Free 1-888-313-2665

Visit us on the internet at http://www.arcadiapublishing.com

On the cover: Meadville is flood prone, traversed by a half dozen streams. French and Cussewago Creeks converge at Mill Run, fed by Dick Run, College Run, Cemetery Run, Neason Run, and other intermittent streams, to carry the plentiful rainfall toward the Allegheny River. This 1913 photograph shows the LaFayette Hotel portico and lower Chestnut Street commercial block, as traffic starts to move again.

David Mead had corduroyed the community's main streets by 1800, and continuing efforts attempted to lay the dust (or mud) to make travel easier. The answer came in late 1889, when bricks were fired to a strength that supported heavy traffic. Soon Meadville's streets were a rosy grid of long-lasting pavement.

CONTENTS

Timothy Alden chose an Adams-Federal style for the 1820 main building of his college. Bentley Hall's presence on the hill set a high standard for the rapidly growing community's buildings. Ruter Hall, a classroom building to its east, and the early residential Culver Hall (inset) followed its lead in pattern and salmon brick construction before the Civil War.

INTRODUCTION

Founded in 1788 by David Mead, a somewhat disgruntled pioneer from eastern Pennsylvania, Meadville is the oldest permanent settlement in northwestern Pennsylvania. Sited near the marshy confluence of a rapid millstream and French Creek, and close to open farmland used by the local native inhabitants, the population grew quickly, attracting Revolutionary War veterans and newly arrived immigrants from the East Coast. French Creek, so named for the earlier French military presence, was the original "highway," connecting the new town with the Ohio River and points south, as well as with the southern shore of Lake Erie and points north.

After the final purchase by the commonwealth of territory from the Iroquois in 1792, land developers moved in to northwestern Pennsylvania to claim those portions of the donation lands that had either been unsettled or abandoned by the soldiers for whom they were intended. Mead's, or Mead's Mills as it was called, became the center for these speculators, the principal one being the Holland Land Company. As in the initial stages of the development of early settlements, the first buildings known in Meadville were of logs, including a defensive blockhouse, the original courthouse, and the Mead family cabin.

By 1804, when Meadville became the county seat for the newly organized Crawford County, the town boasted an economic base of industries such as weaving, tanning, and brick making and a healthy trade network of animal droving and flour and lumber milling. Dr. Thomas Kennedy, who had served with Washington in the Revolution, was responsible, with Holland Land agent Roger Alden, for the laying out of the grid of streets (1795), still the center of town. He also promoted the building of the first bridge over French Creek, an essential element in trade and movement to the west. Timothy Alden, a graduate of Harvard, founded Allegheny College in 1815, bringing higher education and classically inspired architecture to the wilderness.

The Federal style was the first for important buildings in Meadville, which included Bentley Hall (c. 1822), designed by Alden as the principal structure on the college campus. Also designed in this manner was the second courthouse, sited on the public square known as the "Diamond." Gradually new forms found their way to western Pennsylvania, and the Greek Revival style appeared in Meadville. The best surviving example of this is the Unitarian-Universalist Church, dated 1836. Several antebellum homes of prominent citizens of Meadville reflect a mixture of Federal and Greek Revival ideas, including Edgar Huidekoper's Hill Home (1839) and the Baldwin-Reynolds House (1842).

Long forgotten, except for archeological remains, is the canal system of the 1820s–1870s, which provided the Meadville area with greater and faster communication with the outside world. However, the railroad industry proved to be "the most potent factor in the development of the town" in the late 19th century. By the time Meadville was incorporated as a city in 1866, the Atlantic and Great Western Railroad passed through the town and, as the New York, Pennsylvania and Ohio (later the Erie Railroad), established its principal mechanical repair and stores departments before the end of the century. The buildings associated with this early railroad history, almost without exception built of brick, reflect some of the earliest styles of industrial architecture in the United States. The city's mid- and late-19th-century commercial structures also followed the latest trends, including cast-iron columned and porticoed facades.

Spurred on by the new industry associated with Drake's "discovery" of oil in the far southeastern corner of the county in 1859, newly wealthy citizens built mansions to exhibit and celebrate their wealth. Empire Revivals, Italianate Villas, Victorian, and Arts and Crafts "cottages" of immense proportions and a number of mixed breeds all appeared on the scene. Another method of using and exhibiting this new wealth was to support the building of charitable institutions. In Meadville, this included the founding of hospitals (the original two [1870 and 1880] now being combined as a single medical facility) and the Independent Order of Odd Fellows Home (1872), the first fraternally sponsored orphanage in the country.

The earliest religion to form an organization in Meadville was the Presbyterian, meeting regularly before 1800. Their first brick church was erected in 1819, followed by the present edifice in 1875. The Episcopal church, consecrated in 1828, was built in the Palladian form popularized by Christopher Wren over a century before. It was replaced in 1883 by a more fashionable Gothic structure. The Unitarians, then an Independent Congregational community organized in 1825, built their Greek Revival church in 1836. The Baptist congregation, formed in 1831, has had three buildings over the years, ending with the present Richardsonian Romanesque structure of 1904. From 1818 onward, German congregations of Lutheran, Reformed, and Evangelical persuasion have erected buildings that reflected both religious ideas and German cultural practice. The first Roman Catholic community, also German, founded the Church of St. Agatha in 1849. This was followed by the Irish St. Brigid parish in 1862 and the Italian St. Mary parish in 1909. The Methodist Episcopal congregation constructed a church in 1825, and the African Methodist Episcopal Church acquired its first sanctuary in 1850.

The first educational structures in Meadville were sponsored by some of the religious communities. These included Allegheny College, founded by the Presbyterian minister Alden but acquired by the Methodists, with whom the college retains a connection. In 1834, the Pennsylvania state legislature passed the Public Education Act, authorizing public schools for all students. To their credit and the future of public education in the area, all of the 27 districts in Crawford County at the time adopted the law. Meadville itself boasted two ward schools (1868 and 1869). Other early structures for higher education included the original Academy (1805), the new Academy (1826), the Meadville Theological School (1844), and two establishments for female education (1842 and 1846).

The complexion of Meadville's architecture and economy changed in the early 20th century with the development of Talon Zipper, unique to Meadville, and with the presence of the American Viscose. A chamber of commerce pamphlet of the 1950s dubbed Meadville, "the Hub of Industrial America," emphasizing the city's strategic geographical position halfway between New York and Chicago. Talon and the Viscose carried the area through the Great Depression, only to fail in the late 1960s, bringing a very much delayed depression to the community. The nationwide failure of the railway systems also greatly affected the appearance of the city and the well-being of many of its citizens. Modern architecture, promoted by those with what seemed modern, or forward thinking ideas, came into being in Meadville in the 1960s, when many of the familiar buildings of Meadville's past disappeared in favor of shopping malls. An arterial bypass cut the town's center off from its traditional face on French Creek and from the railroad beds that followed the river.

Nevertheless, there is much that remains in Meadville's architectural heritage to admire, to have pride in, and to preserve. Architecture is the ultimate expression of a community's culture. As the circumstances of life within that community change over time, so do architectural forms and materials, reflecting the needs and desires of those who create and use them. Meadville is very fortunate to possess buildings that speak so eloquently of its past.

—Diane Shafer Graham, Ph.D.

One

IN SERVICE TO ALL

The buildings illustrated and discussed in this chapter were all erected in response to the community's needs. City and county legal functions, fire and military emergencies, food distribution, educational and social awareness, and postal communications were addressed by and housed in these structures. Each example not only fulfills its intended function(s) but also reflects its contemporary architectural mode and the ideals that support the use of that mode. For instance, the classical references in Federal, Palladian, Georgian, Colonial, and/or neo-Colonial styles refer not only to the Greek and Roman forms that represent the beginning of Western civilization but also to the structures that represent and embody the ideals and the beginning of American civilization. Other forms, such as the Second Empire, also express human triumph over tyranny. As in their functions, these buildings speak of the community's ties to and belief in our unique national heritage.

—Diane Shafer Graham

Meadville became a borough in 1823 and a city in 1866. In its early years, the borough was run from a docket desk in the burgess's home. The original city hall was built in 1866 and was rebuilt about 1915 in a yellow brick popular in the city. The new building, which withstood the test of 50 years' time, retained the general shape and style of its predecessor, replacing the louvered bell tower with an elaborate turret and the double front stable doors with a columned front entrance. Brick replaced the quoining cornerstone, and heavy keystone lintels appeared over the windows.

The Atlantic and Great Western Railroad's offer to participate in the construction of the 1866 city hall was not selfless. The railroad's wood frame station and yards needed fire protection from wood- and coal-burning engine sparks, and a condition of the cooperation was a fire hall in the city building. Thus, the original city hall had a large bell tower with which to call volunteer and off-duty firefighters and a stable and steamer garage on the first floor, accessing Chestnut Street by two arched doors. The buff brick city hall was constructed at the foot of Chestnut Street in a combination of Federal, Gothic, and Second Empire styles. Its quoined corners and elaborate eyebrow lintels for man-doors and upper-story windows reinforced the notion of prosperity still far from its peak. The city council met on the second floor over the stables, and the city lockup was behind the stables.

Responding to the siren song of urban renewal grants, Meadville razed the 1915 city hall in 1973 and built a new modern fluted concrete and steel column structure at the realigned Arch and Water Streets intersection. The new building incorporated the city administrative functions, police and jail facilities, and the district magistrate office that replaced the former municipal court. The building has expansive north and east window exposure and an open interior floor plan, and it provides an excellent council chamber and meeting room space, as well as room for administrative expansion.

With the arrival of automotive equipment and the rebuilding of many rail yard buildings in brick, the need for an "at-hand" fire brigade disappeared. The city fire station removed to a more central location on Park Avenue, and the horses were put out to pasture. Again built in the familiar soft-yellow brick, the new station included corbeling and arched walls over the second-floor windows. The second floor provided dormitories for the now full-time department, and four vehicles were housed on the first floor. A bell tower remained to announce the fire location and was also used as a drying area for hose. The city recently moved to a new renovated facility, and Central Station has been preserved in a restaurant complex.

The first Crawford County Courthouse was a two-story log structure on the west side of the public square. In 1826, a handsome brick structure, designed by Richardson, replaced it across the square but was quickly outgrown. Following the Civil War, a massive Victorian structure became the third courthouse, combining Second Empire with Beaux-Arts detailing. Both the county administrative work and the court were under one roof, with the third floor behind a mansard roof. The building was symmetrical, with corner quoining and a Doric column portico. Its dome had clocks facing north, east, south, and west and was topped with a statue of Justice, and the building dominated the newly developing park it fronted.

The post–World War II era brought increasing responsibilities to the county level of government, and the 1867 courthouse offered inadequate space. In 1954, the Victorian building was remodeled into a neo-Colonial form, with north and south wings that extended west toward Diamond Park, a dormered third story, and basement spaces made usable for public access. The portico entrance was topped with a Greek entablature and raised to roof the second-story bays. The clocks were retained under a largely symbolic bell tower. The major reminders of the former building are in the marble entrance and transverse halls.

As a result of the War of 1812, the issue of defense of the Northwest became apparent to state and federal authorities. Camping 3,000 militia at Lord's Spring was not an efficient military mode. In 1814, with danger at bay, the state erected an arsenal at Main and Randolph Streets, the intersection of roads to Erie and to Warren, on land donated by David Mead. The building had nine bays on the first story for artillery carriages and space for blacksmiths and gunsmiths to work. A second floor provided storage for military supplies and loading doors for swinging material down to waiting wagons. Never utilized for military purposes, the building provided overflow space for Allegheny College and classrooms for "African" children of the neighborhood under the 1834 and 1854 segregated Pennsylvania public school acts.

Following the Civil War, participation in local militias was no longer required, and they were replaced by state units, later organized as the National Guard. The local arsenal property was converted to North Ward School, and a new site for the armory was found on Diamond Park. The structure was built of brick, probably from the Stoltz yard at Kerrtown, with Dutch gable parapet walls, narrow windows, and crenellation and a single turret for decorative elements. Current plans for consolidation of county units will make this property available, probably for some public use. A special element of this image is the presence of the teardrop electric streetlight, the earliest style used in Meadville.

5466   City Market, Meadville, Pa.

Area farmers had habitually peddled their produce from wagons at street side or door-to-door for nearly 100 years, while residents for nearly as long petitioned for a market house to localize this trade. In 1870, the decision was made, and Market Square became a reality. Originally a one-floor structure five bays long, the brick building featured arched windows and a slate roof with a quatrefoil window at the gable, half-round windows at the apron-roof level, and strap-and-hanger work below the eaves. An elaborate weather vane measured the winds. The structure was an overwhelming success under a succession of profit-motivated market masters, and a second floor and four bays were added in 1917, providing comfort facilities and space for an emerging group of human service agencies. The facility served as an economic stimulator for a marginal city business district and remains today a magnet for the downtown.

The universal appeal of the Meadville Market House is attested to by these two images, taken in 1941. The Meadville Garden Club sponsored a series of shows, or fairs, meant to raise the growers' skills at display and marketing and to encourage additional producers to attend market. In the rare interior shot with winner-featured showcases, the building space still utilizes the early vendor stalls. The exterior view of Market Plaza has been used as an object lesson in business district development. The image shows not only the vendor trucks crowding outside in the early morning hours but also the successful businesses elbowing the venue, among them a restaurant, a newsroom, two meat markets, a plumbing and heating store, Mr. Ellsworth's photography shop, the Cities Service gas station that replaced Krueger's greenhouse, a just-out-of-sight A&P grocery, and the Kepler Hotel and Restaurant—all in a short one-block space.

How seriously education was taken is in a sense measured by the buildings that were purpose-built. The North Ward School, known also as the Dick School, was an elementary school around 1920. Note the brick street, the trolley tracks, and the telephone lines. Built in 1870, the Italianate decorative elements have been maintained with the separate boy and girl entrances, turrets, bell tower, and the elaborate flagpole base much like that at the contemporary market house. At least one addition was built on the east facade behind the front wings. The "new" Centennial High School was built in 1888 and was quickly overwhelmed by the influx of students from families who arrived to meet the demands of an increasing job market. In 1897, the Reynolds School (also pictured here) was opened as a manual arts, or vocational, school. Basically Italianate, it presents a more stripped down, muscular appearance, appropriate for a school that taught foundry and mechanical trades.

The Centennial 1888 High School, a major expansion of the previous Academy on Market Street, met the community's needs only until about 1915. A new high school was self-evidently essential, and this contemporary collegiate-style school opened in 1923. Built as a U around a courtyard facing Diamond Park, with an acoustically perfect auditorium, boys' and girls' gymnasiums, and a full-service cafeteria, the school produced spring and winter graduating classes each year. Reshaped as a junior high and then abandoned by the school district for expansions at the North Street senior high and vocational-technical school complex, the school is now on the endangered building list of Preservation Pennsylvania, with a plan by a developer willing to preserve its essential structure.

Those who work with family history searches in the post–Civil War period often note the number of family units in which children are split up and dispersed among relatives or neighbors or even strangers as a result of the death of a parent. The Independent Order of Odd Fellows sought ways to address this painful social problem and, in 1872, opened a home in which widows or widowers could live with their children and keep their family unit intact. They were enabled to hold jobs and support their family by an Odd Fellows staff that provided child care as needed. The applications grew exponentially, and additions to the facility were made repeatedly, the last in 1925. Described as a Greek Revival, the building was initially a large foursquare frame home on upper Main Street. An addition was built and tied into the existing structure with a wraparound porch and carpenter Gothic, or steamboat Gothic, decorative elements.

The Odd Fellows' Home, Meadville, Pa.   Otto Speakman, Publisher.

Erected on the site was a secondary masonry building, which displayed a Romanesque tendency. The Old Fellows home eventually included a chapel, a shallow swimming pool, a gymnasium, covered porches, and extensive recreation areas to support the family apartments. In the facility's final incarnation, all the previous buildings disappeared and on the approximate footprint of the originals was built a brick, rambling Colonial Revival. Elaborate brick courses, or bonds, were used, and colonnades were introduced to this block-long structure, which managed to avoid, as had its predecessors, any institutional brand. The families raised here developed an extraordinary loyalty and returned yearly for summer reunions. The Odd Fellows order was rightfully proud of the success of the children who routinely went on to successful and normal lives. When the state took over responsibility for fractured and dysfunctional families, the fraternal order's feeling of filling a necessary service faltered, and the orphanage was closed in the 1970s.

Odd Fellows Home of Western Pennsylvania
MEADVILLE, PA.
Oldest Fraternal Orphanage in the World

ESTABLISHED 1872   Cornerstone of New Building Laid July 30, 1928

23

Post Office and Masonic Building, Meadville, Pa.

Post offices were originally, and until fairly recently, temporary addresses chosen by the politically appointed postmasters. In Meadville about 1912, the congressman wrested from the postmaster general a commitment for a federal building, one that would house the post office, as well as offices for federal officials and agencies such as Civil Service and Selective Service. The building was constructed of high-quality materials on the standard Georgian Revival pattern for federal buildings. The lobby featured black walnut carved woodwork, terrazzo floors, and brass grillwork. White marble balustrades underscored the windows and punctuated the roofline, and white granite quoins wrapped the building corners. The signature decorative element was the Palladian windows. A skylight illuminated the sorting room, its well allowing natural light into the second-floor offices.

When the postal service, in 1983, announced its intention to abandon the building for one with additional truck space, the community suffered a severe shock. The facility was customer friendly and conveniently located for patron service. Following an extended period of distress, the local redevelopment authority negotiated an option and a historic easement on the lobby. The authority found a willing buyer who converted the facility into a medical and professional building and kept the major historical elements intact.

1929

In 1923, when the Centennial High School was decommissioned and the new collegiate-style building was erected on Main Street, the Meadville Library, Art and Historical Association evaluated its own position. Adjacent to Centennial High, the consortium had been serving essentially as a support service institution for the schools and receiving Meadville School District reimbursement. In addition, it was becoming increasingly apparent that the old wool mill production structure immediately on Mill Run was not an ideal location for the group's purposes. A major fund drive raised the necessary money, and the consortium moved up across Main Street from the new high school. The library used the full first floor, and the art and historical societies shared the second floor in the Whiting Room and the Shryock Room, using the central room for a gallery-museum area. All three shared basement workrooms. The board chose to adopt the post office Georgian Revival look of red brick with white decorative elements and the highly stylized Palladian windows.

Two

In God We Trust

The principal architectural form of the majority of Meadville's churches, whether Episcopal, Methodist, Presbyterian, United Church of Christ, or Roman Catholic, is Gothic. Variations on the recognized high Gothic of European origin include Norman Gothic, Pugin Gothic, South German Gothic, Victorian Cottage Gothic, and Italian Gothic. Romanesque form is best expressed in the Richardson-inspired Baptist church of 1904, although Romanesque details such as an asymmetrical facade or plan and rounded arch windows may be found on other structures. The chapel form, seen so well on the Baptist and Methodist churches of Wales, existed in the original Baptist church (*c.* 1840), the Central Presbyterian Church (*c.* 1840), neither of which is extant, and in the African Methodist Episcopal church (*c.* 1850). The surviving example of a Greek Revival temple form is the Unitarian church (1836). Whichever style was chosen, whether as a formal architect's conception or as a reminder of the cultural origins of that particular congregation, each structure was dedicated to Christian worship, fellowship, and a sincere trust in God.

—Diane Shafer Graham

In 1825, a small group of members left the Presbyterian Church and formally subscribed 32 members in 1829, when it organized as an Independent Congregational Church. The church was originally supported by Margaret Shippen, a declared Unitarian; Harm Jan Huidekoper, agent for the Holland Land Company; and Arthur Cullum, an early businessman whose son George Cullum, a West Point graduate, drew up the plans for the 1835 church structure. The church was designed in the Greek Revival style after an earlier Philadelphia church. Its columns are Doric, lacking a base, and the triglyph in the frieze has three vertical bands. Pilasters are embedded in the corners of the brick exterior walls. Stone lintels and tall interior-shuttered windows reflect the Adams architectural influence. The interior has well-preserved box pews and limited decorative elements that respect the early commitment to non-distracting ambience.

Christ Church Episcopal was erected in 1826. Newly appointed judge Henry Shippen was introduced to community participation on arrival with his immediate appointment to the building committee, and the cornerstone was laid in 1827. A decade later, the parish building was opened, and in 1878, a rectory was built. The early church, with its entryway bell tower and truncated steeple, reflected the English Village Gothic style, and the parish house and rectory additions enhanced that view. When the congregation decided to enlarge the church in the 1880s, the Gothic style remained predominant, while Romanesque features enriched the imposing facade. An elaborate rose window dominates the gable, the bell tower rises in a pointed steeple, and decorative details enrich the exterior—dentils, hood moldings, gables, hip knobs, and Byzantine crucifixes. Double lancet windows and plate tracery are special features of this church.

The latest of the Diamond Park–facing churches built was the First Baptist. This 1905 church replaced an earlier Federal-style church on the west side of Walnut Street. Oral tradition says the new church was built, at least in part, to accommodate the Revere Foundry bell bought by Deacon Boileau. Apparently, the steeple of the old church was not strong enough to support the tolling of the great bell. To confirm the authenticity of the bell and to purchase it, Boileau traveled to Washington, D.C., where the bell had been hanging in a Baptist church that was torn down to make way for the Ford Theater.

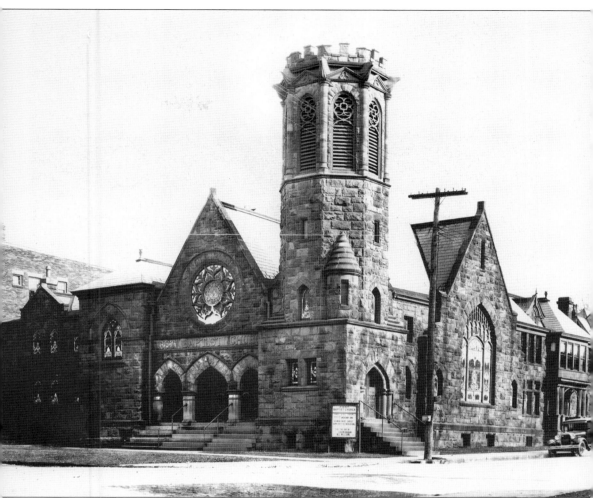

The new church draws on the Richardson Romanesque style and may be a pattern-style church for northwest Pennsylvania Baptists. Its bell tower is substantially reinforced and topped with a crenellated parapet. Its arcade-style entry is dominated by a rose window, and a stained glass skylight illuminates the sanctuary. The architectural style is carried into its adjoining Sunday school, meeting rooms, and administrative offices.

The Stone United Methodist congregation was established in 1806 by Methodist circuit riders. When it was built in 1825, the church became the hub of an active French Creek circuit. As the home church for Allegheny College after 1842, Stone United Methodist played a major role in the community, with a large and stable membership that included many community leaders. The 1860s photograph documents the beginnings of the conversion of the public square from a drovers' corral and militia parade ground to a central park and ceremonial area. The 1930s picture shows the rebuilt church following the disastrous 1927 fire. The parsonage has been moved to make way for Kingsley Hall and Sunday school rooms.

These two pictures, taken by Keystone View stereo cameras, dramatize the horrendous fire of 1927. Firefighters from neighboring towns were called in to assist in controlling its potential spread to the adjacent Masonic building, Unitarian and Baptist churches, and nearby residences. In the rebuilding, the church's lancet windows, small buttresses, and stained glass windows—characteristic of English Gothic Revival—were all replicated.

Meadville's congregations first held their meetings in the 1805 courtroom and then moved to the Brick Church, built by the Presbyterians in 1820. The church's 80 pews accommodated small to large congregations. Services were scheduled to meet the needs of circuit riders of all faiths. As the town grew, congregations built their own churches, but the Presbyterians continued to provide meeting space and to maintain the town's cemetery.

Today's Presbyterian church was built on the Brick Church site in 1873 in English Gothic Revival style, with an asymmetric layout. It embodies the decorative elements of the period, with trefoil windows, offset dentils, hood moldings and double lancet windows. The church features two towers, a bell tower and a spire tower, both richly ornamented. Extensive Sunday school, administrative offices, and meeting rooms have been added over the years.

St. Paul United Church of Christ, organized as the St. Paul Evangelical and Reformed congregation, began meeting in 1842 with like-minded, German-speaking Lutherans in a frame church on Poplar Street and in 1866 built their first brick church at Park Avenue and Poplar Street. The present church was built in 1910, a reflection of the cohesive German community that provided merchants, metal workers, teachers, brick makers, and artists to the city. Gothic buttresses and lancet stained glass windows wrap the yellow brick facade. An asymmetrical entrance at the base of the bell tower, with its lancet louvred opening, rises to a crenellated parapet. Triptych stained glass windows center each gable parapet.

Built as the Bethany Protestant Episcopal mission of Christ Church, today's Wadsworth Avenue Evangelical Church was an expression of the growth of Vallonia, a railroad worker's community organized as a borough in Vernon Township in the post–Civil War period. With the presence of the nascent Keystone View Company, Meadville Rye Whiskey distillery, and a full array of community services, Vallonia seemed ready to follow in the footsteps of Kerrtown and Fredericksburg, other developing communities on the west bank of French Creek. However, the location of Meadville's water fields triggered Vallonia's annexation by the city. The church structure was a pattern church for rural mission churches. The board-and-batten structures featured simple Gothic lines and often handsomely decorated interiors. Like most of Vallonia, the church was in a frequent flooding zone.

Although Roman Catholic congregations had formed at Crossingville, Frenchtown, and Rome Township early in the county's history, Meadville's first Catholic congregation, the Church of St. Agatha, was formed in 1849 with the influx of German immigrants. It sponsored the inclusive German School, attended also by German Lutherans and Evangelicals, all of whom formed a cohesive neighborhood in the South Meadville area. The church was built in a southern German style: a brick structure with elaborate stained glass windows and a "lace" steeple flanked by turrets.

The St. Agatha interior, even more than the facade, reflected the ornate styling of southern German churches, as seen in this gaslit view of the sanctuary. The massive pulpit and delicate communion rail demonstrate the sophisticated wood carving skills, and the stations demonstrate the congregation's native preferences. Recent modernization by a more diverse congregation has simplified and lightened the interior of the sanctuary. The altar scene demonstrates the effect achieved. St. Agatha was soon followed by St. Brigid, as Irish immigrants resisted the continuation of German language services, demonstrating that Catholics, like Protestants, agreed to disagree over doctrinal and other issues. At one point there were 40-plus congregations in the city of Meadville.

An early Mother Bethel church of the African Methodist Episcopal denomination was established in the 1850s. The black community had congregated as early as 1821, when a Sabbath school report notes participation of 20 "colored" members and two instructors. This building had been built by another congregation (reports vary as to which) and was remodeled following the Civil War, again in 1908, and again in the pre–World War II period. The central entrance was moved north, and a bell tower was added at the northwest corner. Probably at the same time, stained glass was substituted for the clear panes. In the 1870s, the church was the site of meetings that challenged the state's 1854 segregated-school law, and a suit by member Elias Allen resulted in the desegregation of Pennsylvania schools in 1881.

Three

ELEGANCE AND EXUBERANCE

New ideas in domestic practicality, charm, and splendor came to Meadville, as they did to other communities, through local knowledge of accepted practice or as expressions of financial success by the newly wealthy. The earliest substantially built homes were either frame or brick in the Palladian, Greek, and Classical Revival styles associated with the Federal and Jacksonian periods, with regular, balanced facades and plans. These were the homes of Meadville's land agents and citizens of industry and law. Commercial success, including that associated with the oil industry after the Civil War, brought the introduction of very grand revival styles, such as the Italianate Villa, Second Empire, and Queen Anne, all very decorative with asymmetrical plans and imposingly large windows, porches, and towers. Pattern-book homes, including Craftsman bungalows, and simply built public housing became popular after 1900, as the demands of a growing population of more limited means were addressed. Meadville's residential architecture is as varied as any American community of its age and size and fluctuating prosperity.

—Diane Shafer Graham

This five-bay Federal structure is reportedly the first brick residence in the city. It was built by James White, an early tanner whose pits were along the adjacent ravine stream shared with Samuel Lord. Following White's death, the property went through a series of owners and was eventually bought by William Reynolds, who had taken over the adjacent Baldwin mansion. Reynolds gave the house to his daughter Fannie when she married A. C. Huidekoper, and history was written. The White house closely fronted the Terrace, and the young couple made many improvements—the glassed-in west porch is most evident.

As the family prosperity increased, and spurred by the example of father William Reynolds at the Baldwin mansion and of the Little Missouri Horse Company Huidekoper brothers at Conneaut Lake, Fannie and A. C. Huidekoper decided to move the house up the hill and enlarge it by over-building around it. The resulting impact of an immense chateauesque home with its parapet Dutch gable, portico, decorative buff brick work, and porte cochere is exceeded on the interior by a two-story paneled entrance great hall with encircling balcony, a charming retention of the White house's wainscoted and window-seated parlor with Dutch-tiled fireplace, and an elegant dining room overlooking the back gardens through stained glass and leaded windows.

The Huidekoper family's success story began in Meadville with the progenitor Harm Jan Huidekoper's arrival as an agent of the Holland Land Company. He married Rebecca Colhoun and built a relatively modest frame home that he called Pomona at the south extreme of Water Street just outside the village limits. The house, a five-bay Adams-style Federal building with typical decorative features, had balancing wings north and south and a wrapping nine-bay veranda. As the family grew, an added working ell was added on the east side. The Holland Land Company offices were immediately to the north, a brick two-story structure. Son Frederick Huidekoper removed Pomona, damaged by a fire, and built a massive Victorian mansion in its place before leaving the increasingly industrial neighborhood for upper Chestnut Street.

The Shryocks were successful merchants. The first arrival, Daniel Shryock, made a tidy fortune converting brine from Beaver Township wells to salt for the frontier communities. When an unlucky decision to deepen the wells and increase production struck oil in 1819, the family settled in Meadville and operated a variety of businesses, most recently the home furnishings store on Chestnut Street. Located on the Terrace, the Shryock home was a Victorian Italianate with a viewing tower overlooking French Creek. The western facade is sheltered by a neo-Colonial porch with balustraded second story, and the south facade features a large, light-capturing bay. The third half story is well lit with a series of paired eye windows.

Following the death of early settler Samuel Lord, his Mount Hope plantation was acquired by Henry Baldwin, a U.S. Supreme Court justice. Baldwin and his wife, Sally, intended to spend their semiretirement years in the town where he had first begun the practice of law and where his wife had an extended family. He designed his house after Hunter's Hill, a Nashville mansion once owned by his political guru, Andrew Jackson. An antebellum Classical Revival house, it followed the British pattern of first-floor public rooms and second-floor parlor and library. A veranda with stacked Doric columns wrapped the four facades at two stories. Tall double-hung windows with interior shutters increased both the interior light and the ability to control interior temperature.

When William Reynolds acquired the house from his aunt Sally, he set upon a course of improvements, with walnut and bird's-eye maple woodwork, satin glass door lights, parquet flooring, and a charming proscenium arch for the rear parlor, which showcased musical at-home evenings. Today special events such as the Trees of Christmas continue the tradition of hospitality at the Baldwin-Reynolds House.

The house and three-acre parcel was acquired by the Crawford County Historical Society as a county museum. In 1976, a time capsule country doctor's office was moved from Little's Corners north of the city to the former stable level to the north. Listed on the National Register of Historic Places, this small National-style structure had spent nearly 100 years in the side yard of Dr Russell Mosier. It came complete with Mosier's records, pharmacy, equipment, taxidermy collection, house call bag, driving gloves, voltammeter, and adjustable examination chair.

The property had always been serviced by an artesian spring at the brow of the hill, and a springhouse served to refrigerate perishables. In 1870, when the French Creek Feeder Canal was closed, cut stone was salvaged from a waste water weir and used to build an icehouse with slatted interior walls, using cooling Conneaut Lake ice and insulating straw.

Originally a second-floor parlor with a privacy nook, this room became the master bedroom under William Reynolds's remodeling. Featuring tiger maple woodwork elaborated by "ears" at the windows, the room is paired on the right across a dressing room space with Henry Baldwin's former library, which has similar upgraded woodwork. This room is maintained by the Antique Study Club, members of which made the needlepoint rugs. The furnishings represent a number of periods of county history.

This view through the three south parlors of the first floor illustrates the design elements that make the museum interesting. The near room, with its marble fireplace, is furnished in a combination of the Second Empire and high Victorian styles of the three generations who occupied it. The acanthus-leaved corbel springer at the archway opening represents William Reynolds's upgrading of the house, as do the elegant gaslight chandeliers, seen in the octagonal center music room, created when Reynolds built central heating ducts into the interior walls. The far room showcases the enclosed veranda section and stage area, which allows a small walnut-paneled library to do double duty for entertaining. The parquet floor of the third parlor is just visible.

The McClintock-Fuller House is a product of the wealth that came to the county through the discovery of oil in its southeastern corner at Titusville. This high-style Second Empire Victorian with its gingerbread decorated rakes and stone hood moldings is composed of common bond red brick. The most prominent original feature was the central tower, since removed. The decorative fish scale slate roofing has been retained, but the ironwork cresting has been removed. The floor plan seems disjointed by contemporary standards, but impressive woodwork again testifies to the hardwood reputation of the region. Staircases and pocket doorways still glow. The third-floor space presents a small proscenium arch intended for home entertainment, and a commercial addition at the rear is unobtrusive.

Hill Home was built by Harm Jan Huidekoper's son Edgar Huidekoper, as the family removed from the Water Street home grounds. It appears as a Classical Revival with the later addition of the semicircular portico. In its earlier incarnation, it offered a more Adams-style appearance. Its third-floor clerestory offered additional light and access to a rooftop observation area. The elaborate cast-iron fencing came from the Philadelphia ornamental iron foundry of Evans Shippen, the brother of Edgar's wife, and remains today a street side reminder of Victorian elegance.

This pair of houses was built by the Roueche family from a Barber pattern book. The larger family home is Queen Anne Eclectic. It is an outstanding example of the high Victorian style available to successful merchants of the period, with its detailed masonry chimney, spindle work, boxed and bay windows, tower, and gables, as well as its stained glass windows and balcony-verandas. The house has tucked under its wing a small Eastlake Stick, reportedly the mother-in-law house, built on the same parcel of land. City records show that the utilities, water, and sewer all ran to it through the main house meters. The mother-in-law house, with its elaborate porch spindles, gable sunburst, and bay window bull's eyes, competes discretely with its neighbor's effusive decorative detailing.

The current owner of the home has lovingly emphasized the decorative elements of this Stick Victorian-Eastlake house. It is an exceptional presentation of the early English half-timbering tradition revived by Downing. The decorative shingle styles, the window bays and half porch-balcony spindles, and the eave detail are highlighted by paint color and emphasize the rosette and flute woodwork. The house makes a statement of the upward mobility of its builder.

Residence of General Mead, founder of Meadville, Pa.

Built in 1796 as a New England farmhouse, the General Mead house was renovated in the early 1900s by the DeArment family. Added were the classical portico with its decorative swags, the porch, the balcony, the porte cochere, and the leaded glass windows. The entrance hall and stairway were retained. Today the house is undergoing restoration.

This Queen Anne Eclectic, recently renovated, adds to the streetscape of Chestnut Street. With its tower, elaborate gable, and busy roofline, it presents a transition from the half-timbered Stick style to the more elaborate Queen Anne, which is slightly masked by the modern porch replacement.

The Isaiah Alden House, on Liberty Street, is one of the earliest frame survivors. Isaiah Alden, a relation of Timothy and Roger Alden, joined them in Meadville as a land developer. From the placement of its second-floor windows, the house appears to have had an addition to its original Adams-style structure on the north end. A number of extensions appear on its east, or backyard, facade.

Also on Chestnut Street is this Craftsman Eclectic, with its remodeled gable porch roof partially obscuring the central eyebrow window. The wraparound porch disguises the cross-corner windows, which were intended to let more light into the interior, and the hip roof implies a bungalow intention. The spindled porch is hidden by over-height plantings, somewhat distorting the home's proportions.

In a departure from the single-family and extended-family homes most common to the city, the Hillcrest development was constructed at the city limits in 1937. This is nationally the first Federal Housing Administration project, built by the Meadville Housing Corporation in response to the exponential growth of Talon Zipper and American Viscose. The plan was designed on a hillside, laid out with communal garages at the end of each short block and varying family-sized space in an American Folk style, with gable front or I-house design. The development is still owned by Meadville Housing, which has limited the remodeling and renovating, retaining largely the original vision. Playgrounds, tennis courts, and a water tower were built into the plan, and a footbridge linked the children to the nearby East End School.

Four

HIGHER EDUCATION ON THE HILL

As the oldest continuously operating college west of the Appalachian Mountains, and as a selective private institution, Allegheny College (1815) possesses a microcosm of changing architectural styles and tastes. From the mixed Palladian–Greek Revival architecture of Bentley Hall and that of Ruter Hall, through the Second Empire of Hulings Hall, the Romanesque of Montgomery Gymnasium and Ford Chapel (with Gothic details), the Beaux-Arts of Reis Library, the Renaissance Revival of Carnegie Hall, the neoclassical of Arter, Brooks, and Cochran Halls, the modern of Pelletier Library and the Campus Center, to the postmodern of the science and physical education complexes, each structure celebrates and reflects both the college's connection to the outside world and the generosity of loyal alumni and concerned patrons. Allegheny's students are exposed to the highest standards of education in the classroom and to some of the finest examples of America's architectural heritage around the campus.

—Diane Shafer Graham

Lord's Gate was erected as College Street, the main traffic entrance to the campus, was shifted to the rear of Bentley Hall. It honors Samuel Lord, who donated the Susquehanna and Waterford Turnpike acres of his Mount Hope plantation to the projected college. Its Federal-style cornice, Victorian lamps, and Greek scroll bracketing reflect the diversity of the campus architectural styles.

Bentley Hall was planned by Timothy Alden, probably from an early pattern book, to be the central hall for his "Harvard of the West" on the nation's new frontier. Its three floors and basement were to house quarters for the president, recitation halls, and, on the third floor with a wonderful view of the valley, the precious library he had so carefully assembled from East Coast bibliophiles. Begun in 1820, Bentley Hall was completed around 1830 by David Dick, who assumed the task of finishing the founder's dream. This early-20th-century view of the hall, facing the old path of College Street, defines the Federalist-Adams architecture: the east and west wings with their porticos, pilasters, and keyed lintels; and the Federal entrance with its fanlight topped by Palladian windows at second- and third-story levels.

This early stereo view by Dunn documents how, over time, plantings were added to soften the hillside, walkways were paved, bridges were constructed over ravines to connect newly added buildings, and rhododendrons were planted to enhance the course of College Run southwest to French Creek. The towering scroll-bracketed cupola bell tower was shuttered to protect the bell that was rung for classes and then lit to provide a focal beacon for the campus. Today the bell is silent, but an electronic carillon replaces it.

The second building on the campus was Ruter, its simple Federal lines reflecting the Greek Revival period in its gable entablature. It was built to encompass a chapel, recitation rooms, and a laboratory. Its stark lines in an increasingly Victorian world led it to be called affectionately "the factory." The building was named to honor the college's second president, who led the Methodist accession and then left for the far western frontier to work as a missionary.

This view of the west facade of Ruter features the softening effects of plantings and highlights the pilasters and pediment of the Bentley-facing door, which led into the original chapel space.

As enrollment grew and students traveled from distances to attend, the demand for dormitory housing increased. Two oilmen stepped forward. Culver Hall offered housing for male students but burned in 1882. Marcus Hulings donated money for female housing after women were admitted in 1870. His substantial building grew with the addition of Brooks Hall in the pre–World War II period and of Peiffer and Walker Halls in the post–World War II period.

Caflisch Hall, a dormitory built originally for men, demonstrates the mixture of styles that dominated early-20th-century campus buildings. The Greek Revival portico, the Federal-style windows with keystone lintels, the Roman arches over the door transoms—all topped with a Spanish-style tile roof—sample the styles of the campus.

As the school approached its centenary, the college under president William Crawford was growing vigorously, and a massive building and development campaign was undertaken. The resultant buildings followed no architectural nexus. Reis Library, with its purpose-built Treasure Room for Alden's library, skylit atrium, open and closed stacks, and reading room with special collection areas, was built in the Beaux-Arts tradition. From acanthus leaves to Corinthian columns, the building declared itself as the treasure house of the campus.

To meet the expectations of the 20th century, Alden's college launched itself into intercollegiate athletics. Montgomery Gymnasium, of English Fortress style, contained a basketball court and swimming pool and fronted a walled and gated football field.

Addressing the increasing interest in the physical sciences, Newton Observatory was placed between the new science building and the new chapel. Its mobile, copper-domed roof and excellent telescope made the heavens available to the serious student and for years introduced community school classes to the skies. The effort to blend into the campus landscape included the neoclassical entrance, its columns supporting a portal entablature.

Andrew Carnegie was generous in his funding of both libraries and educational science facilities. Thus, south of the observatory, Carnegie Hall marked the southern limits of the campus. It reflects the Italian Renaissance impact of the early 20th century. Arched brick structural bays combine with relief sculpture. Arched bays for first-story windows rise to paired casements, the whole being capped by a hipped, Spanish Mission red tile roof.

Sited just north of the observatory and south of Ruter Hall with its existing chapel, Ford Chapel was built in an elaborate, massive Masonry Tudor form. North and south interior walls are dominated by stained glass, and the apse presents small, arched stained glass studies. The east window over an interior balcony features a rose, or rosette, window. The slated roof is steeply gabled, and in recognition of the college's new emphasis on music, an oratory provides rehearsal and recital areas overlooking the ravine. The heavy bell tower contributes to a Romanesque quality and heightens the building's impact on its North Main Street placement.

Sarah B. Cochran Hall was built in an Italian Renaissance style that reflected the donor's home on the Monongahela River. A Doric order colonnade faces Main Street, flanked by Palladian windows. Quoins wrap the building corners, and a rhythm of modillions and a red tile roof complete the Italian flavor. The building has recently undergone extensive restoration to become an alumni center.

Charles M. Stotz published in 1936 a defining study of the early architecture of western Pennsylvania, during the course of which he became enamored of the Greek Revival-Federal, or Classical Revivalist, architecture that had survived here. His retention as Allegheny's architectural adviser explains the prewar and postwar architecture of Allegheny's campus, as his book had influenced much of western Pennsylvania's public architecture. Arter Hall, with its columned portico, transom window, and classical entablature, "bookends" the ravine with Bentley Hall, its modest cupola echoing that of the 1820 building. This classroom building included a basement-level stage house with excellent facilities for mounting the elaborate productions that became part of the college curriculum. An adjacent scene shop was built for production work.

As the number of women matriculants grew to match men through education curriculum and music emphasis, more dormitory space was created. Initially it appeared as a series of extensions to the original Hulings Hall. All three of these accretions—Peiffer, Brooks, and Walker Halls—reflected the Colonial Revival architectural image. Brooks Hall reached back to include the Victorian Dormer styles at the fourth-floor level, but its primary east facade included the portico, entablature, Palladian window colonnade, and eyebrow lintel upper-story windows that face Lord's Gate, the primary traffic entrance to the campus. The building included a central college dining room and public lounges, as well as a central switchboard, women's gymnasium, and dean's suite.

The final addition to the Hulings complex was Walker Hall, again Colonial or Classical Revival in impact. The traditional facade enclosed a modern dormitory that included shower and laundry rooms and Pullman kitchens in lounges. The basement included mechanical rooms for the Hulings (now Brooks) complex and support rooms for the adjacent dining room. Its east facade overlooked the upper ravine and the Darling Arboretum, natural features that made on-campus living desirable.

Despite its massive proportions, old Reis Library, with its dark brick Beaux-Arts style and winding approaches, never dominated the campus. Its entrance, featuring corner quoins, acanthus-leaved lintels, and ornamental brackets, is a neoclassical portico accessing a skylit octagonal atrium that augments the stacked windows, which provide natural light throughout the structure. Its central location in the 20th-century campus made it a well-used meeting and study site for the student and faculty populations.

As the college moved into the postwar period, additional building began to move toward the International architectural style. South Hall dormitory, which embraced the old Alumni Gardens, with its flagged plaza, fountain, and dining hall, stretched to face Bentley as it delineated the southern limit of the campus. To its east, Pelletier Library linked the original campus to the extending new campus, using brick paving and walls to create a commonality through material, as the architectural style became increasingly modern.

Five

IN FOR A PENNY, IN FOR A POUND

The intention behind the early grid pattern of Meadville streets was that the public square would become the commercial and institutional center of the town. However, businesses gravitated to the lower, or western, end of Chestnut Street, as being closer to the pathways of, first, French Creek, second, the interstate canal system, and, subsequently, the railroad lines. The large number of hotels in this central area (no hotel exists in downtown Meadville today) indicates the importance of Meadville to the trade, shipping, and travel industries. The late-Victorian character of the commercial structures along Water, Chestnut, and Market Streets and Park Avenue (not on the original plan) reflects the post–Civil War prosperity of the town, brought by the railroad, oil, textiles, and metals manufacturing industries. The updating, or modernizing, of those Victorian facades expresses the mid-20th-century wealth brought by the zipper and synthetic fiber manufacturers. Today the railroad is of minimal importance to local business and has been replaced by an arterial bypass, which promotes the growth of drive-up retail outlets in suburban areas. The downtown center of the city is currently fighting to stay alive, partly because so much of the architecture that made it attractive to citizens and customers is no longer there.

—Diane Shafer Graham

In the late 19th century, the commercial district on Chestnut Street expanded exponentially. The corner of Chestnut and Market Streets captures a diverse and well-invested series of primarily Italianate Victorian buildings, which house a drugstore, real estate office (note the cross-corner door), the Lyceum Theater behind its portico, and a plumbing and heating dealer, whose elaborate facade includes a third-story Palladian window and a second-floor bay window. Frisk's confectionery dispensed iced creams in the buff brick building. The Park Avenue Congregational Church and the Academy Theater competed for space and attendance. In evidence of gentler traffic flow, a cyclist stops in the intersection to exchange greetings with a pedestrian. Passersby were tempted by the aroma of roasting peanuts emanating from the strategically parked wagon. Some 40 years later, the south side of the same intersection (below) has begun to show the impact of modernization: the corner building has been replaced by a Chicago Modern yellow brick building, which, however, retains a cross-corner entrance; the elegant Veith Building has been remodeled with black Carrera glass storefronts; insulbrick and Chicago-style windows and a buff brick Beaux-Arts infill; and loudspeakers hang dumbly, waiting for carol time. The street front has lost its cohesive self-image in a dash for modernity.

Little architectural detailing is apparent in the storefront of the National Meat Market. The Victorian kickboard and the ventilating transom window are work-a-day features. Decoration appears in the deer "columns" and the rabbit "dentils."

Vernier's furniture store was one of the companies that opened around Market Square. The store's large-paned windows provided natural lighting, as well as display space for a wide variety of goods. Simple iron bracketing provides support for the overhang balcony, which serves the rental rooms above.

One of the city's early hotels, at the corner of Center and Water Streets, the Central Hotel, with its five-bay facade and its extended ells, represents the early effort to maintain the quality of buildings while meeting new needs. The Central's handsome recessed entrance with elaborate transom and its somewhat homey shuttered windows kept it a better-class boarding hotel into the 20th century. Reading the picture, however, one gets the feeling that nice young ladies did not walk down that side of the street unescorted.

Thurston House presents a boarding hotel out of the center business district, where county and country travelers might feel comfortable. Sylvester "Vet" Thurston, the county's well-traveled balloonist, kept this home base. Thurston had moved to the city from Guys Mills and a small inn to the Crawford House, a stage stop and courthouse-attorney's stopping place on Diamond Park, before settling down in this homelike building.

The Delamater Block, built in elaborate Italianate Victorian style and topped by a Federal pediment above the cornice, was constructed with oil money from the Noble-Delamater well. It housed retail firms on its first floor, including telegraph offices, drugstores, and jewelers over the years. Its south-facade portico led into an ornate lobby and grand staircase to the hotel on the second floor. Eventually, it acquired the small Halsey Hotel to its north and incorporated it. In 1955, the building burned in a spectacular fire, the loss of its Kiltie Bar and business lunch restaurant dislocating the daily pattern of the business community.

The community rallied to the loss of its last surviving hotel with the purchase of Hill Home, a fine neoclassical structure left empty by the death of its widowed and childless owner. Contracting with the Treadway chain, the backers built an in-town motel, with high-quality rooms, dining room, and community meeting rooms. Today the building survives as an assisted living community. The remaining evidence of Edgar Huidekoper's Hill Home is the elegant cast iron fencing along the street and an arborvitae-shielded garden walk in the back.

The Bates Company, on upper Chestnut Street, specialized in music, from sheet music to pianos. The building featured an elaborate Flemish bond brick soldier course, bricked arched lintels over single-pane windows, and luxfor lights around the facade display windows. This early-20th-century view is unique in its display of both horse-drawn and automotive delivery. The slender, well-decorated building to the west housed the Knights of Columbus on the second floor and Knorr's grocers at street level. Both buildings survive today, with the Knorr building lovingly restored.

The repeating reinvention of Market Square began in 1870. This view features the second Kepler Hotel, fronted by verandas and crowned by pediment signboards. Beyond it Muckinhaupts Livery reflects the pride in structures taken by even mundane businesses.

A view of the businesses that crowded in around the 1870 Market House confirms the city father's faith in their initial investment. From right to left are the first Kepler Hotel, a frame countryman's boarding hotel; Vernier's secondhand furnishings; Haas' meat plant; a plumbing purveyor; the office of the Conneaut Lake Ice Company; and Mr. Ellsworth's photography studio. All built within 10 years of each other, the Victorian consistency lends a nostalgic ambience to the scene of the horse auction at the Market House.

The impact of the Market Square commercialization shows in this picture of the razing of a Victorian home to make way for the Kepler addition. The remaining gable-screened, slate-roofed residence, with its handsome chimney forms, soon gave way to a storefront building, and the herringbone brick sidewalk gave way to cement. Seen in the distance is the power plant, which made streetlights and trolley cars a matter of fact.

A hardware store and a tire service apparently shared this fairly elaborate Park Avenue building, once occupied by the *Crawford Journal*, for many years the newspaper of record for the county. Again designed for street side retail with upper stories taken by lodges and nonpublic access businesses, the building has decorative notes that include prominent hooded moldings and cornice end brackets with hip knobs. The style is generally Romantic Italian, characterized by two-over-two window lites. The broadside for the Charlie Chaplin movie is obviously newly posted.

Meadville's first skyscraper and likely its first elevator appeared to the south of the Market House in 1912. The Crawford County Trust Company was the convergence of two banks and offered professional office space on its upper floors. It was intended to make an impact in a booming economy. Patrons were greeted by a Chicagoesque first-second floor row of pilasters; more Italianate features rise above, the building corners emphasized with quoins and a parapet probably shielding the mechanicals at the roof level.

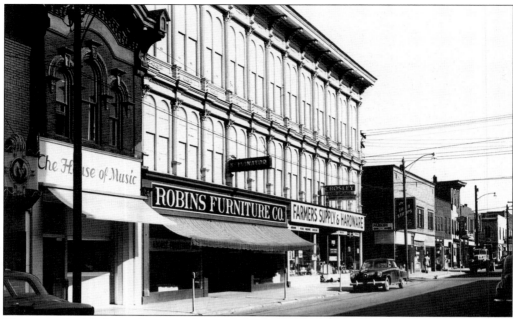

The nosey Studebaker and gooseneck streetlights replacing the earlier torchieres date this view of the Water Street commercial district as the early 1950s. Again the 19th-century architecturally important buildings overwhelm the marginal investment replacement buildings that housed S&H Green Stamps and yet another Western Union location. The House of Music has "modernized" the street-level floor of a Renaissance Revival Italianate bank building, and the Mead (movie) Theater, home to Ma and Pa Kettle, presents its neoned marquee on another old buff brick building.

Farther south on the street, the Delamater Savings Bank building, with its Romanesque and Gothic arches and upscale masonry construction, is razed, with the abutting retail spaces offering a view of the insul-stone covering used to hide rather than restore the multiuse structure, the only alternative to deconstruction seen at the time.

Pharmacies early moved into the soda fountain business to assuage customers as they awaited their prescriptions. "Big" Wirts, on Chestnut Street, enhanced the wait with a rocky road sundae and, still further, with candy and small gifts. As were the interiors of most retail stores, Wirts was built with dark woodwork, high tin ceilings with cooling fans, and secure display cases, which gave importance to their contents. Mosaic on the front of the fountain allowed for artistic expression—and, perhaps, ease of cleaning.

In Meadville, Western Union was heavily used at the beginning of the 20th century to transfer urgent news or urgently needed dollars. The clock was the arbiter of the exact time. Decorative touches were considered unnecessary, perhaps even inappropriate. Note, again, the tin ceiling, the exposed display of technology, and an early fluorescent light fixture, probably replacing pendant fixtures. As the commercial district moved east on Chestnut Street, the fine Victorian Italianate architecture moved with it. Here the Diamond Grocery, now Hunter's News, displays its pressed metal parapet detailing and spires. At the corner, the unusual frame Second Empire Derickson home stands next to the commercial building that housed the law offices of the family, and across the public square, now firmly identified as Diamond Park, the Crawford Hotel welcomes its last guests before being razed to make way for the new First Baptist Church.

Built in 1885, after fire destroyed the Opera House, the Academy Theater was a fully staged live theater venue designed by J. M. Woods of Chicago, a nationally known theater design specialist. It presented live shows—from drama and opera to oleos and vaudeville—welcomed flickers and later movies, and had both an orchestra pit and a theater organ. In the 1980s, challenged by television, it was threatened with closure and saved by a community willing to work to bring it back to live theater productions. A varying series of marquees were placed over the sidewalk to tempt passersby inside. Relief sculptures atop the pilasters gave clues to the artistic flare of the interior. An odd little gable parapet sits above the cornice work, while arched windows denote an Italianate style.

A larger movie theater, the Park, was built in 1922, staged for vaudeville shows only, but with twice the seating capacity of the Academy Theater. The theater displayed extensive decorative elements on ceiling and walls. It was built as an infill behind the corner at Park Avenue and Chestnut Street, with a Chicago Beaux-Arts store building filling the retail opportunity on the street-facing corner. Wall sconces and chandeliers illuminate the interior to display the post-Victorian paneling filled with stenciling and wallpaper patterns of the age.

The 1959 flood put Meadville on national television and served as the trigger for a rich archive of photographs on the downtown at a fulcrum point in its history. This view from Market Street east up Chestnut Street revisits the Market Street to Park Avenue block, as it gives a rare view of the Park Theater marquee, slimly inserted over its Chestnut Street entrance.

Cluttered and over-signaged as it is, this 1924 southward view of Water Street conveys a commercial shopping energy to gladden the heart of any merchant. From Nash cars and trucks to Humphreys cleaners, Endicott-Johnson shoes to the Delft restaurant in the St. Cloud Hotel, horses and cars and trolleys delivered the customers.

When the Shryocks' salt wells in Beaver Township struck oil, the family shifted gears to retail furnishings and household goods and built a handsome store on the corner of Mulberry Street. Three levels of display windows only just began to suggest the stock, and the triptych window at the fourth-flour level confided that tents were made there. These Italianate features are accompanied by a partial frieze and crenellations at the corners of the building. Recently, the structure was given a reuse for senior housing and remains a part of the Chestnut Street scene.

The Kepler Hotel was the last of a long series of hotels by five generations of a hospitality family. The Keplers had operated a turnpike inn in Woodcockboro, a plank road hotel at Venangoboro, an oil rush hotel at Titusville, and two county seat hotels in Meadville before "Sam Bill" Kepler built this brick Federal-style building with its Folk Victorian verandas around 1890. The decorative woodworking was characterized by spindle work and thin brackets typical of the 1870–1910 period and presented a welcoming appearance.

Each year the Kepler family sponsored a reunion dinner for members of the Grand Army of the Republic–Civil War veterans and their wives and widows. This high Victorian private dining room must have offered a homey ambience to veterans and family members. The hotel served the community for nearly 100 years and was recently renovated into senior condominium units as part of a Business District Action Plan (BDAP) revitalization program for the city.

Masonic Building, Meadville, Pa.

In the same period that the Meadville Federal Building and the Crawford County Trust Company building were constructed, the Free and Accepted Masons constructed a lodge that was to be partially supported by professional office and first-floor retail space. The style is influenced by Richardson's design for Chicago office buildings, but it is primarily an Italian Renaissance building with a Beaux-Arts cornice wrapping the facade. Ionic pilasters both harken back to Greek temples and support the massive lintel beneath the cornice. Tuscan capitals above the pilasters feature a rivet carving, honoring Meadville, "the Tool City."

Taken from a crane at the south end of Diamond Park, this view captures the survivors of nearly 200 years of building in the downtown. The strong brick construction and the classic styles have helped retain, on the south, the Masonic lodge, the 1912 Federal Building, the Flood and Spirella Buildings, the First National to Sun Drug block, and the Shryock store; and on the north, the Derickson-Ralston Block, the Bates and Knorr and Academy Buildings, the Woolen Company to the Eldred Building, and the Trust Company to Smith Clothiers. Solid building blocks all, they are in place, awaiting another century of service.

Six

HOOKLESS FASTENERS AND GET-A-GRIP PLIERS

The service manufacturing of early Meadville—such as tanning, lumber and flour milling, and cloth and brick making—gave way after the Civil War to various heavy industries. Beginning with local ore and coal deposits, foundries of iron and bronze soon made use of the expanding rail lines to import raw materials and export finished goods. The largest single industry (and employer) of the 20th century was Talon Zipper, having as many as seven plants working at one time. The American Viscose Company, which made rayon and other synthetic fibers, came second in the employee population. Both companies were out of business in the city by 1987. Along with Channelock Pliers, a family-run firm, newly created tool-and-die works have today earned Meadville the handle of "Tool City." Light industry has contributed its part to the city's manufacturing scene through companies that include the Spirella Corset Company, lost to changing fashions; the Keystone View Stereopticon Company, living on in a museum mode; and Dad's Pet Products, also an original Meadville company still run by its founding family. One should not forget, as many employees of other industries did not, the Meadville Rye Whiskey distillery, whose brick buildings stand waiting for adaptive reuse, while the resurrection of others such as the Viscose plant has already taken place.

—Diane Shafer Graham

This cosmeticized picture of Athens Mills, by local artist Alphonse Fugagli, romanticizes the booming lumber industry of the region but accurately records the clerestory roofline, multiple windows for light, and location on French Creek and the Feeder Canal. The area's outstanding hardwood production was an early basis of industry from the day David Mead put his sawmill on this same site and began rafting lumber to the Pittsburgh markets.

A more realistic image of operations appears in this early-20th-century Dock Street (Mead Avenue) stave mill. Carew was a well-known cooper by 1877, and his firm had joined with Collom's in vending wood scraps and coal for heating in the "nothing goes to waste" philosophy of the period. Typically, little money was wasted on prettifying the workplace, and random additions met short- and long-term needs.

With small amounts of iron ore and coal available in the county, Meadville had become a foundry and metal center in its early industrial development. From Torbett's nails through David Dick's eccentric gear press and the Atlantic and Great Western Railroad Foundry, the town had developed a core of skilled labor. Consequently, it was not surprising that the William H. Page Boiler Company chose Meadville as a manufacturing center for its industrial and commercial boilers. Locating a site near the freight station, the company built an open quadrangle building, one story, with puncheon wood floors.

In its last manufacturing expansion, Talon Zipper took over the Page building and added an interior three-story structure to accommodate development and production of new lines. Talon added a modernization feature of sawtooth rooflines, which allowed better natural lighting, but retained the wooden puncheon floors. The hybrid building was the last zipper production line in Meadville to close.

1914

Talon itself had opened in 1914 in a modest barnlike building on Race Street, as it set out to transform Whitcomb L. Judson's bulky hookless fastener into a streamlined garment closure. From this very small beginning, the firm moved into and out of a dozen structures around the city, as demand for its product slowly grew with improvements.

As the product approached general acceptance, an opportunity to centralize the operation rose with the removal of the Meadville Theological School to the University of Chicago. Three Meadville Theological buildings at the junction of Arch and Alden Streets offered needed space for corporate headquarters and development activities, as well as extensive land for the building of new coordinated manufacturing and production lines. Hunneywell Hall, the Meadville Theological refectory, was an imposing building in Classical Revival–Beaux-Arts style, evidenced by heavy quoins, a Palladian window, and a portico. The front-facing gable gave a regal character to the Arch Street facade.

As a master of marketing, entrepreneur Col. Lewis Walker incorporated impressive building signage and landscape techniques into the development of his "industrial park" and used the high-class visuals in advertising and sales materials. The detailed view of the art deco water tower is reminiscent of merchant estates in Florence, Italy.

The company built behind this office space an extensive yellow brick factory keyed around a tall water tower fashioned like a campanile, with loading and service facilities on the Pine Street side. The building was punctured with multiple windows of all shapes, including a sawtooth roof, seen to the east. The former campus was well landscaped and, with its clean and quiet industry, blended into the existing middle-class residential neighborhood.

At least a small part of the company's success must be credited to a sense of humor. As this widely published cartoon indicates, it was all right to have fun—an attitude that did not hinder the company's effort to create zippers for snow boots or for space suits. It is perhaps just possible to discern the twinkle in the eye of founder Col. Lewis Walker in his official portrait. Walker was an Allegheny College graduate and the lawyer for the G. B. Delamater family, members of which had struck a gusher on Oil Creek and gone on to become bankers and philanthropists. When Walker happened upon Whitcomb L. Judson and his hookless fastener invention, capital was available for the risky venture.

Meanwhile, across the street from Page Boiler, another success story was growing, as the DeArment family's Champion Tools broke into international markets on the strength of the newly developed Channelock pliers. This 1929 photograph catches the firm at its conversion point from a farrier's and automobile toolmaker to an artisan's toolbox supplier. The separation between administration and production is quickly recognizable; the building in the foreground is rather more formal, appropriate for conducting business.

Not all Meadville's industrial growth related to foundry work. In the 1890s, B. Lloyd Singley, a "mature" student, applied to Allegheny College. He earned his tuition money as a canvasser for stereographic cards and viewers, and with the help of his new father-in-law (a railroad machinist) and the advice of his sister-in-law (a teacher), he found he could improve his income by producing and marketing the product himself. The Keystone View Company started in the family home at Vallonia and eventually became the largest stereo maker in the world, moving into the old Centennial High School building when the school there closed.

The Keystone View Company closed in 1971, due to a combination of television and computer competition. Today a fascinating and massive collection of Keystone's recreational and educational materials is on view at the Johnson Shaw Museum. The museum, a charming structure, began life as the office of the Huidekoper Land Company, successor to the Holland Land Company. It had a brief use as a magnet elementary school, and then, appropriately, became for many years the home of the First Church of Christ, Scientist, B. Lloyd Singley's denomination. Its early Classical Revival features are seen in the vaulted portico, a modillion-lined gable, and an arched window with eared hood molding to divert water.

Built originally for the Chautauqua Press, this building was acquired by the Spirella Corset Company. M. M. Beeman had found the answer to the breakage problems of boned corsets with a flat metal intertwined stay that was flexible. The company marketed its products through corsetieres who visited customers at home to measure them in privacy; the garments were then sewn in Meadville. This crenelated castle provided office space, well lit by large Italianate windows. The corbeling reflected a common element in Meadville brickwork. The near building in this picture is a production building of the Meadville Woolen Mills. It was converted into a facility for the Meadville Library, Art and Historical Association (MLAHA), and part of its space was used for the support services provided by Spirella to its young women seamstresses. In addition to using the MLAHA collections, the company provided an infirmary, organized a travel club, published an employee newsletter, and sponsored a Class A baseball team, maintaining the stadium for community use.

The success of the company required additional buildings. This north-lit sewing facility had classrooms and demonstration and sales rooms on the first floor. When the labor pool was found to be inadequate for the production needs, the business moved to Buffalo and to Canada, and the building converted easily to furniture store showroom.

46. Phoenix Iron Works Foundry, Meadville, Pa.

The Phoenix Ironworks began its operation on the basis of David Dick's eccentric gear press and grew into a major foundry. It was an early producer of gasoline engines, furnaces, and a wide variety of metal products. Built tall to provide space for the movement of ceiling cranes, these buildings often also required a clerestory for additional ventilation of the foundry-generated heat. Capitalizing on its underlying deep alluvial gravel water base, the town in 1929 welcomed the arrival of American Viscose, an early producer of rayon fiber. Built as a nearly self-sustaining community, the plant prospered through the prewar and World War II years. Few industrial operations occupied as much of the landscape as seen here in a plant that is designed to serve the function of the production line. Facing overseas competition it could not beat, as well as environmental challenges, it became a publicly owned consortium for industrial development.

PLANT OF
AMERICAN VISCOSE CORPORATION
MEADVILLE, PA.

Building on its experience in producing dispensing equipment, the Beman Automatic Oil Can Company moved from producing pumps that would draw vinegar or molasses from basement storage to grocery salesrooms and into the careful housewife's container. Its new market was the care and feeding of the automobile, safely drawing gasoline from underground storage tanks through filters and measuring devices to the curbside car. It became an increasingly prosperous business, but no funds were ever wasted on fancifying the frame shack it operated from. The facility followed barn building practices, even providing a barn-type cupola. It remained in operation until the 1950s.

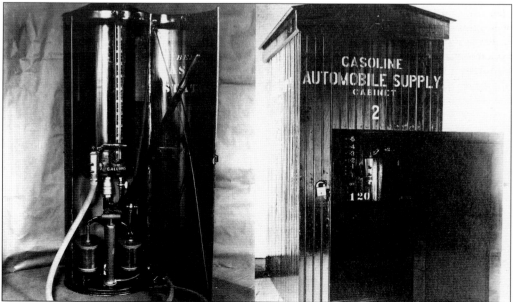

Seven

CREEK, CANAL, RAIL, AND HIGHWAY

George Washington passed by the future site of Meadville, noting in his journal its wide plains, as he trekked along French Creek to confront French troops at Fort LeBoeuf (now Waterford). French Creek, now recognized as an environmental asset, was not entirely navigable, so that docks at Meadville could only operate during seasons of high water. In the drive to open westward travel and trade from the western end of the Erie Canal in western New York State to the Ohio River and Pittsburgh, a system of local canals was devised, including the French Creek Feeder Canal, which passed directly through Meadville. Motivated by easier transport and the needs of the Civil War, the Atlantic and Great Western Railway (later, the Erie Railroad) came to Meadville, en route from New York to Chicago. Regular road travel to points west was facilitated by a series of bridges across French Creek, beginning with Dr. Thomas Kennedy's covered toll bridge, a replica of which is now being nostalgically considered. Many of the carpenters and stonemasons responsible for the canals and bridges contributed their skills in other areas of Meadville's architectural heritage.

—Diane Shafer Graham

In the 1860s, William Reynolds brought the railroad to Meadville. Built by British engineer Thomas Kennard and financed by McHenry's British and Salamanca's Spanish money, the work moved ahead throughout the Civil War. The line ran on a wide-gauge track and covered a hotel station with extensive amenities to encourage its passengers to travel in comfort. The 1864 artist's conception generally matches the 1869 photograph of the completed Meadville terminal. The Atlantic and Great Western office, station, and hotel were built in a high Gothic style of board and batten, bearing William Reynolds's trademark of quatrefoil windows and delicate spires. Pictures of the hotel dining room reflect the Gothic design emphasis. The rail line ran from New York City to Chicago and included spur and loop lines to local soft coal fields and the oil region, ensuring its prosperity.

As the center point on the Atlantic and Great Western line, Meadville was the site of the major rail shops and roundhouse. The rechanneled French Creek and this view from the hill west of the city demonstrate the care taken to provide efficient operation. The roundhouse is centered between the foundry and car shops to the north and the station and business operation to the south. Small living quarters, usually reserved for foremen and operational personnel, are set along Atlantic Street and Great Western Street in the complex.

A 1930s aerial view looking westward gives evidence that the basic layout has survived the intervening 70-plus years. The new cut for the channel of French Creek runs close to the foundry; the creek continues to try to rise in its old bed to the east. The H-shaped locomotive barn, carpenter shops, and foundry remain in their basic relationship to the roundhouse. The major change is that almost every building has been rebuilt in brick.

In 1905, the day-to-day business of the railroad, now reorganized as the Erie Railroad, was still conducted at the station. At the north end, the passengers approached from McHenry Street. The south end housed the freight station and dormitory space for shift workers. The structure still reflected its importance in gable screens, teardrop brackets, and Eastlake detailing. The Railway Express Agency freight service building has been built to the east of the station.

In a 1915 view, the passenger station presents its elaborate chimney style, coursed brick detailing, luxfor gable window, baggage portico, and extensive glazing. The roofline continues to sport its finials. The waiting passengers seem to be mainly male.

While the previous views of the station appear work-a-day, the view from the city side demonstrates an effort to be an attractive neighbor to Meadville's main street. An extensive park, well planted and with an imposing fountain playing, with paved walks leading to the city hall and Chestnut Street retail district would seem to mitigate the disappearance of the 1869 covered platforms, dining room, and hotel. In one of its last hurrahs, the station welcomed a vanishing event: a barnstorming whistle-stop for the 1952 presidential campaign. Architecturally, the station has been stripped to its bare bones, but the trackage looks well maintained, and the trucks are lined up at the Railway Express Agency depot. Looking into a sea of faces, Richard Nixon promised a season of prosperity for the small communities of the nation under an Eisenhower administration. Just 15 years later, the station was razed to make way for an arterial highway.

The memories remain. This "evidence" picture was taken to show the condition of the Mead Avenue crossing on an October day in 1917, when a furniture truck and a yard engine disputed the crossing. A crossing guard occupied the booth to be on hand to manhandle the protective crossing arms into place when a train was on the move. A bench and chair indicate it is an active crossing booth, not built for comfort.

The office of the general foreman demonstrates the privileges that go with responsibility. On the second floor of the locomotive building, from left to right, general foreman T. I. Cole, Loren Curtis, and Thomas Lyons have made a pleasant home away from home. If the building was not built with their comfort in mind, it nevertheless could be homey. When the building was cleared of its contents 80 years later, the drafting table and desk were in still in place; the geraniums and wandering gypsy vine were gone.

8831. Erie R. R. Shops, looking South, Meadville, Pa.

Looking southward around 1915, this closer view of the yards shows a wide assortment of cars awaiting attention. The roundhouse and the turntable made maneuvering in crowded yards feasible. The two buildings on the right have recently been restored and are in use for education and employment agencies. Railroad men were incredibly loyal to their line and their division. When Meadville celebrated its sesquicentennial in 1938, veterans and active railroaders joined to build a replica of the first train to travel through the city. Old No. 5 of the Atlantic and Great Western Railway, built exactly to scale and with an accompanying station, made the route of the grand parade on a flatbed and today occupies a place of honor at the annual Roundhouse, often accompanied by the last living of its builders.

The photographer was documenting the laying of the trolley tracks about 1890, but as he captured the men and boys sidewalk superintending, he caught a rare picture of the St. Cloud Hotel and the early-20th-century Water Street buildings beyond it, including a livery no doubt soon to be out of business as a result of the newfangled "cars." The St. Cloud shows its side residential entrance and its front restaurant entrance, with an ornamental iron railing on its second-floor balcony. Two elaborate Italianate buildings with hooded moldings, both likely banks, and a heavy linteled Federal three-story merchant's building are caught in the cameo.

Trolley No. 7, said to have been the first Meadville street car, is aimed at the carbarns, apparently with the help of the team of horses. In any event, it drew a crowd to the carbarns and station house. Less than 25 years later, this interurban car and the new bus service look set to race. The coach easily won the contest. More flexible in its routing, requiring no overhead lines or tracks, and needing no more service or administrative space than the trolley station house, it depended only on the public roads already supported by the growing number of car owners and was heavily subsidized by the automobile manufacturers.

Moving goods in northwestern Pennsylvania had been a continuing problem since back in 1788, when David Mead walked in, leading his pack animals. Wet weather made for muddy roads, which bogged down wagons. Snow and cold made for ice and isolation. The initial answer was for canals—wasn't the Erie Canal an economic wonder for New York State? Certainly mills and foundries grew up alongside the French Creek Feeder as it passed through Meadville.

Canals were prone to maintenance problems, were only as fast as the mules that pulled the boats, and froze in the winter. They required bridges at every turn and crossroads, most especially in cities, as seen here with Captain Dickson's boat, tied up near the North Street bridge. They had to be dug, clay lined, and counter drained for the cross streams. They needed dams, locks, full-time lock tenders, and retaining walls for canal-side property owners. At several points the French Creek Feeder ran parallel with French Creek itself, as seen below. The commercial traffic apparently had no negative effect on residential housing decisions along it—the town had, after all, long built its homes on the banks of French Creek itself. Here the Shryock House overlooks the dual waterways.

In center city, this canal basin, immediately before David Dick's home, is seen as a sculling practice area. The canal is approaching a conjunction with Mill Run, where the two then flow jointly for about two blocks before separating. The canal was built on a single topographical elevation to avoid the need for locks; Mill Run needed its current to service its mills and reach French Creek expeditiously.

While canal construction was largely invisible once the water was let in, there were elements where stonework and carpentry were visible and impressive. This rare view of the aqueduct, taken in winter, highlights the cut stonework—the product of local quarries—and the carefully constructed conduit that carried the canal water and the boats across the living water of French Creek.

The stone was cut from quarries in ravines along the route. So precisely was the work accomplished that, without mortar, the walls still stand as reminders of the course of the canal and the craftsmanship of the stonemasons. Wastewater weirs, lock and bridge piers, and base channel floors are available for inspection. Camps of up to 200 laborers have been identified in records along the course of the canal to its junction with the main Beaver and Lake Erie Canal at Summit. The closing of the canal for commercial traffic in 1871 did not put an end to its use. Water still remained in its course, and recreational boating was a popular Victorian pastime. This board-and-batten building, probably the home of the boat livery owner, was built on the canal just north of Meadville. Picnic outings up to the Bemus Dam, the original entry into the canal from the creek, were especially popular with college students and sparking young couples.

The image of the first Meadville bridge exists only in a painting. According to old records, early turnpike access to Meadville was by ferry. Following several accidents with loss of life and property, Dr. Thomas Kennedy invested in a covered bridge to access the Mercer and Pittsburgh pikes. The bridge's maintenance was covered by tolls, and the wooden bridge lasted into the final decades of the 19th century. Today a Baltimore truss, painted bright blue and spanning the same crossing point, still takes traffic out through Kerrtown to the Mercer-Pittsburgh corridors and to the Ohio-bound roads that followed the old American Indian trails.

Another covered bridge spanned the creek upstream at Dock Street to access the west side and Cussewago Creek mills. When the Atlantic and Great Western Railroad was built, traffic in the area increased, and the maintenance became a burden. There were also complaints about the "bandits" who lurked in its dark corners and about transients who set up housekeeping in it. When high waters came, the surrounding area was tricky, as this *c.* 1867 picture indicates.

The Dock Street (now Mead Avenue) bridge issue was eventually solved, after an almost two-year discussion, with a cast-iron Whipple double truss bridge. Pricey for the time, it was sturdy and easy to erect and has survived heavy usage since 1871 to the present. This view shows its relationship to the rail yards, Cullum House, and mills.

As motor-driven interurban trolleys and heavier motor vehicles took to the roads, a Baltimore truss was added to cradle the Whipple bridge and extend its capacity. Today the bridge is in the Historic American Engineering Record, a rare survival of early metalwork bridges.

With more motorized traffic moving in the city and the urban trolley lines extending into residential areas, more bridges were required to cross small streams and to ease hill climbs. This bridge, a concrete structure built over a culvert, crosses Mill Run upstream at Grove Street. Note the bricks piled along the sides to complete the paving to the new standards. It is also interesting to see the light fixtures that grace this elaborate city street crossing. The teardrop streetlight visible at the top of the hill dates it to very early 20th century.

As public bridge building became more sophisticated, recreational bridges harked back to simple wooden and log structures. Shown on the Allegheny College campus (above) are ravine-crossing bridges of a type still maintained today and the 1938 Works Progress Administration bridges built in Shady Brook Park and playground along Mill Run. The Shady Brook project was an added enhancement to the Hillcrest Federal Housing Administration development at the city's east boundary for the family-age population increase.

Meadville's public water was drawn from the deep glacial alluvial deposits that underlie the city. In the early years of the system, water was largely pumped by a series of pump houses along French Creek, some to reservoirs and some to water tanks. This pump house is on Clark Street at the south end of the city and speaks to the safe depth of the underground reserves, as it lies almost directly on the line of the freight yards.

In the first half of the 20th century, as the city grew farther and farther up and out from French Creek, the need for a more efficient and modern water system was accepted. A large water field was known to exist under Vallonia, and the city purchased the property. A pine plantation, planted by the Boy Scouts, was put in place over the field, controlling future development to appropriate limits. A community picnic area with picnic tables and water landscaping was created, and the area became known as Waterworks Park, or Ellsworth Park.

In 1905, the city invested in a large single pumping system capable of turning out an amount that could more than serve both the present and future residential and industrial needs of the city. In the 1930s, this neo-Colonial building, characterized by its Georgian 12-over-12 windows and its keystoned lintels, was constructed as an administration building.

ACKNOWLEDGMENTS

The authors gratefully acknowledge their access to the 26,000 images of the Crawford County Historical Society archive. Their appreciation and gratitude also go to Diane Shafer Graham, who has so kindly lent her expertise to our text; Larry Wonders, the historical society's image curator, who helped find each picture we knew had to be there somewhere; our summer work-study students, Marjorie Leinbach, Lura Parker-McGlynn, and Kayla Moyer, who assisted in the clerical and time-consuming tasks that are part of any publication; and Jonathan Miller—without his camera eye and visual talent, no illustrated work would tell its story so well.

Entrance to Greendale Cemetery, Meadville, Pa.

In 1854, a new cemetery was mandated when the state legislature ruled that burials could not be made within city limits. Greendale, a site just east of the city's boundaries, was chosen, and a handsome parklike ground was laid out with rhododendrons, winding roadways, and appropriate amenities. A full-time and permanent superintendent was appointed to keep the grounds, supervise the burials, and maintain the records. And in keeping with the character of the town, a grand gateway was erected, with a central carriage arch and two flanking pedestrian ways. To the end, architectural excellence surrounds Meadville's residents.